DATE DUE

Booms and Recessions in a
Noisy Economy

ROBERT E. HALL

Yale University Press

New Haven and London

Published with assistance from the Kingsley Trust Association Publication Fund
established by the Scroll and Key Society of Yale College.

Designed by James J. Johnson. Set in Electra Roman type by The Composing
Room of Michigan, Inc. Printed in the United States of America.

Library of Congress Cataloging-in-Publication Data

Hall, Robert Ernest, 1943–
  Booms and recessions in a noisy economy/Robert E. Hall.
    p.   cm.—(Arthur M. Okun memorial lecture series)
  Includes bibliographical references.
ISBN 0-300-04857-2
  1. Recessions.   2. Business cycles.   3. Equilibrium (Economics)
4. Macroeconomics.   I. Title.   II. Series.
HB3711.H263   1991
338.5'42—dc20   90–44179

The paper in this book meets the guidelines for permanence and durability of the
Committee on Production Guidelines for Book Longevity of the Council on
Library Resources.

10 9 8 7 6 5 4 3 2 1

To Anne Elizabeth Hall

Yale Class of 1993

Contents

Figures

Preface

It is an honor to help commemorate Arthur Okun's many contributions to macroeconomics. I cannot say that he would have approved of everything that I will say here, any more than he fully approved of the various papers of mine that went through his detailed scrutiny at the Brookings Institution in the 1970s. I can say that Art would have welcomed a debate on these topics, would have taken all viewpoints seriously, and would have made many helpful contributions to my work. Even when Art disagreed with me most vehemently, he never failed to suggest improvements in logic and exposition. He was always on the side of sound economics.

The ideas in these lectures have been taking form in my mind for a number of years. Since 1985 I have been working on a research program on the macroeconomic implications of imperfect markets, and the influence of that work will be obvious. My interest in intertemporal substitution has been much longer standing, though the idea that increasing returns augments intertemporal substitution is relatively new.

I can trace the awakening of my interest in temporal agglomeration specifically to Valerie Ramey's dissertation, and I am grateful to her for many helpful discussions of this topic.

Peter Diamond's and Richard Rogerson's ideas have also had an important effect on my thinking on this subject. Russell Cooper offered additional help on this point during his visit to the Hoover Institution in 1987–88.

The London School of Economics and the Massachusetts Institute of Technology provided opportunities to present early versions of these lectures. Mark Bils, Olivier Blanchard, Jeffrey Miron, and many others in those audiences provided helpful comments.

Steven Durlauf, my colleague in the Department of Economics at Stanford University, was enormously helpful on the noise measurement issue. Our discussions led to a joint paper on this subject.

*Booms and Recessions in a
Noisy Economy*

Introduction

Macroeconomics is a close relative of regional economics. Along a line drawn from New York to Los Angeles, the level of economic activity is hardly uniform. In principle, the regional economist ought to be able to predict the agglomeration of activity at certain points: coastal areas with good harbors, river locations, and regions with unusually favorable living conditions. In fact, however, much of the spatial pattern of economic activity appears to be accidental and arbitrary. The macroeconomist looks at the variation of activity over time rather than over space. Output should be concentrated in the more favorable times. The macroeconomist has about the same level of success as the regional economist. Output is higher in times when the economy is more productive and when the need is most acute, as in wartime. But there is a great deal of apparently inexplicable noise in the variations of output over time.

This book concerns the agglomeration of economic activity over time. From the start, macroeconomists have sought to identify the moving forces of aggregate activity and to describe the economic mechanisms that translate these forces into changes in employment and output. I shall discuss both issues. Some moving forces have distinct identities and are accepted as fundamental by almost all economists—military spending is the leading example. But other moving forces—and apparently the most important ones—are not fundamental. Rather, they appear within a given model as *noise*, that is, as departures of economic behavior from the structural relations of the model. An economy experiences macroeconomic noise, for example, when (1) consumers spend more than would normally be expected given their earnings, assets and the interest rate, (2) businesses spend more on plant and equipment than is warranted by sales and the interest rate, (3) the public holds more money than the customary relation to income and the interest rate, and (4) the stock market values business earnings more it usually does.

Tracking down noise has evolved into a major research program involving dozens of macroeconomists. It cannot be separated from the topic of propagation mechanisms, because noise is the residual in a structural equation. Quantifying noise requires at least a minimal set of identifying assumptions about the structural equations of the economy.

The first chapter begins by setting forth a basic model of temporal agglomeration resting on thick-market effects. Economic activity is more efficient when concentrated over space or over time. Most production occurs in geographic hot spots and takes place between 9:00 and 12:00 in the morning and 1:00 to 5:00 in the afternoon. Employment and output are substantially higher in July, August, and September than in January, February, and March. The thick-market efficiencies that encourage the concentration of activity during certain time periods may be either internal or external to the firm. When they are internal, the firm can make efficient arrangements to take advantage of the effects. An episodic schedule of output is optimal, provided that workers' dislike of such schedules is not so intense as to offset the thick-market effects. The firm should occasionally martial all its forces in bursts of activity; at other times—at night, on weekends, during the winter—the firm should rest. An interesting, unsettled question is whether efficient agglomeration calls for periods of intense effort and periods of rest at lower frequencies. If so, some part of the business cycle might have this interpretation.

When thick-market effects are external to the firm, the possibility of indeterminacy can arise. Externalities involving the density of customers, workers, and suppliers are obviously important in geographic and diurnal agglomeration—midtown Manhattan is the most efficient location in the world for selling cameras, but not in the middle of the night. Within certain limits, the time pattern of activity is indeterminate with thick-market externalities. A recession may be a period during which each firm is relatively inactive as a result of high costs related to low densities of customers and suppliers. Density is low precisely because other firms are in the same situation. A boom occurs when some minor force energizes many firms simultaneously. The boom is self-sustaining because of the complementarity of output across firms. The pattern of recession and boom will appear to be noise to the macroeconomic observer.

In the second chapter I consider the evidence on noise, particularly spontaneous shifts in output originating in the business sector. I develop a simple two-component decomposition of the movement of real gross national product (GNP). One component is the path that GNP would have followed in order to deliver the volume of goods and services actually chosen by consumers, government, and the rest of the world. The second component, noise, is the residual between actual GNP and the theoretical calculation. The two components are roughly the same size, but noise has more power at higher frequencies. Noise is an important part of the business cycle but not of the longer-term variations in GNP.

In the third chapter I set forth a simple general structural model of aggregate output, the interest rate, and the price level. The core of the model is the determination of the level of output as a product-market equilibrium, either competitive or oligopolistic, possibly indeterminate because of thick-market externalities. Monetary nonneutrality can affect either product demand or product supply. In either case, monetary policy has leverage over output as well as over the price level. I develop a two-diagram analysis intended to replace the aggregate demand–aggregate supply diagram.

I hope it will not escape the reader's attention that I do not try to make a case for one existing school of macroeconomic thought over another. In fact, I am struck by the similarity in the analyses offered by the two major schools active today. According to Prescott, Lucas, Sargent, King, and related authors, output fluctuates because the labor demand curve shifts along a flat labor supply curve. According to Akerlof, Stiglitz, Ball-Romer, Taylor, and related authors, output fluctuates because the labor demand curve shifts along a flat locus that replaces a steeper labor supply curve owing to efficiency wages or other considerations. Even the institutional specialization that used to separate the schools is breaking down—some of the most important work on temporal agglomeration is being done at the University of Chicago by economists trained at the Massachusetts Institute of Technology.

ONE

Noise over Space and over Time

The spatial concentration of economic activity is no mystery to economists. Let there be costs of moving products from one place to another, and producers and consumers will locate close to each other. Along a line drawn almost anywhere on land, economic activity (GNP per square foot) will vary by many orders of magnitude. Agglomeration tends to occur at natural ports and other salient geographic points. But because the distribution of economic activity is probably close to indeterminate, the location of economic hot spots is largely a matter of historical accident.

The distribution of economic activity over time is the subject of macroeconomics. Agglomeration over time involves the same principles as agglomeration over space and occurs at a wide range of frequencies. Over the day, activity reaches pronounced peaks in the morning and again in the afternoon. Over the week, the weekend is a trough. Over the year, activity gradually rises to a peak in early fall and then collapses in winter. Every two to ten years, there is a contraction of several percent in real GNP in the form of a recession. And the economy has important movements at even lower frequencies. In the United States, activity was high in the late 1940s and early 1950s, low in the late 1950s and early 1960s, high in the late

1960s and early 1970s, low in the latter half of the 1970s and early 1980s, and has been high since then.

Until very recently, the models developed in formal macroeconomic analysis did not have properties conducive to temporal agglomeration. On the contrary, their assumptions about preferences and technology compelled smooth distributions of activity over time. Consumers prefer a smooth consumption stream to one with a higher average but significant variability over time. Workers likewise favor smooth work hours. A technology concave in labor input produces a higher average level of output for a given average of labor input if production occurs at the same level at all times.

All the facts about temporal agglomeration contradict the standard formal model. Until recently, macroeconomists have had two main ways to resolve the contradiction. One is to invoke a sufficiently powerful driving force within the neoclassical model so that it will predict realistic output volatility in spite of the forces tending toward smoothness over time. This strategy defines the real business cycle school. Their models posit large vibrations of the production function to explain observed agglomeration at business cycle frequencies. The natural tendency for concave preferences and technology to generate smooth output is overcome by large variations in the productivity of work effort in boom periods compared to slack periods. The corresponding approach to spatial agglomeration is to explain higher output per square foot in Manhattan as against Iowa by assuming that land in Manhattan is hundreds of times more productive than land in Iowa.

The second view considers the standard neoclassical model to be a longer-term growth model. Deviations from the smooth path of output are the result of some kind of coordination failure or price rigidity. Efforts to put this type of model onto a firm theoretical basis have not appealed to a wide class of economists. The second view attracts many adherents among macroeconomists, however, because they find the alternative of the real business cycle model so unconvincing.

Recent thinking points in a direction that retains important parts of the neoclassical apparatus yet generates realistic outcomes. The essential idea is to drop the concavity of technology but to keep the concavity of preferences. New models of temporal agglomeration explain the irregularity of output as the victory of efficiencies of producing output in occasional batches over the cost of irregular work schedules. Unlike the real business cycle model, the new model based on increasing returns does not deny the cost of irregular work; that is, it does not assume that labor supply is highly elastic.

One important source of increasing returns and temporal agglomeration is the thick-market externality described by Diamond (1982), under which the costs of doing business are lower in places, or in times, of higher total activity. For example, it is cheaper to sell cameras in midtown Manhattan than anywhere else in the country because the density of camera buyers is so high. Buyers are dense because Manhattan is a major emporium for goods of all types and because there is a wider selection of cameras at much lower prices than anywhere else. In the temporal setting, costs are lower in booms, because higher activity makes markets thicker.

Increasing returns need not derive from an externality in order to make temporal agglomeration efficient. Rogerson (1988) introduces a simple form of increasing returns—workers incur a fixed cost each day they go to work. Specialization into days of intense work and days of no work is optimal, even if preferences would favor spreading work over all available days, absent the fixed cost. Rogerson's model explains an important form of temporal agglomeration, the concentration of work into the five-day workweek. His model also makes a contribution to the understanding of temporal agglomeration at lower frequencies, a topic I shall return to later.

Murphy, Shleifer, and Vishny (1988) offer a model, also founded on increasing returns, of once-and-for-all temporal agglomeration. In their model, if all industries adopt advanced technologies simultaneously, enough income is generated to cover the fixed costs of every industry. But income effects are not a good candidate to explain temporal agglomeration at business cycle or higher frequencies, because of permanent income considerations. Research in progress by the same authors considers episodic temporal agglomeration.

1. SIMPLE MODELS OF AGGLOMERATION

Thick-Market Externalities

Consider an economy comprising many firms, indexed by i, in many units (spatial or temporal), indexed by t. Let y_{it} be the output of firm i in unit t, and let Y_t be the average output of firms in unit t. There is a single factor input, labor, and the common level of labor input for all firms in unit t is x_t. All firms have the same technology,

$$y_{it} = g(x_t, Y_t) , \qquad (1.1)$$

where the presence of Y_t recognizes a thick-market externality. The production function is increasing in x and Y and is concave in x and in Y separately, but not jointly; there is a region where $g(\theta x, \theta Y)$ has an elasticity greater than 1 with respect to θ. Then

$$Y_t = g(x_t, Y_t) , \qquad (1.2)$$

which can be solved for Y_t,

$$Y_t = f(x_t) , \qquad (1.3)$$

where $f(x_t)$ is the maximum level of output that can be produced with x_t.

In a spatial setting, where t runs over geographical units, it would be natural to put a constraint on the sum of the x_t:

$$\frac{1}{T}\sum x_t = \bar{x} . \tag{1.4}$$

That is, whatever labor is available, $\bar{x}$, can be allocated across the geographical units. Each person would work in only one place; it is reasonable to exclude the possibility that some could achieve a higher level of satisfaction by spreading work over many places. In the temporal setting, just the opposite holds. Concentration of all work in one period might yield far less satisfaction than spreading the same amount of work over many periods. In principle, the analysis needs to deal with preferences defined over all periods, for goods and work. To keep the discussion simple, I shall assume that individuals allocate hours of work according to a utility constraint,

$$\frac{1}{T}\sum u(x_t) = u(\bar{x}) . \tag{1.5}$$

Here $u(x)$ is decreasing and convex. There is no substitutability between goods and work, but there is some substitutability between work in one period and work in another, depending on the convexity of u.

Because of the externality, a free-market economy will not generally achieve the optimal schedule of activity. If the production function $f(x)$ has sufficiently increasing returns to scale to offset the curvature of $u(x)$—that is, if the output-utility set $\{(y, v) \mid y \leq f(x) \text{ and } v \leq u(x) \text{ for some } x \in [0, 1]\}$ is nonconvex—then the optimum would involve switching back and forth between two levels of employment. Although the decentralized economy will not usually operate at either of these points, it may achieve some of the benefits of agglomeration through a regular cycle of activity.

I define a *periodic equilibrium point* as a level of employment that equates labor supply to labor demand at a level of employment different from the benchmark level, $\bar{x}$, in the labor supply constraint. That is, x is a periodic equilibrium point if

$$\frac{\partial g(x, f(x))}{\partial x} = -\lambda u'(x) . \tag{1.6}$$

where λ is the shadow value of utility in terms of goods. If the economy cycles through a set of periodic equilibrium points, all sharing the same λ, and satisfies the labor supply constraint, then the points and associated frequencies make up a *periodic equilibrium.*

Absent the thick-market externality, equation 1.6 and the labor supply constraint will have the unique root $\bar{x}$ and $\lambda = -(\partial g/\partial x) / u'(\bar{x})$ and stable employment at this level will be optimal. The externality makes possible multiple periodic equilibrium points, because the marginal product of labor can be an increasing function of labor input, x. For example, if

$$g(x, Y) = xY^\gamma \tag{1.7}$$

and

$$u(x) = \frac{(1 - x)^{1 - 1/\sigma} - 1}{1 - 1/\sigma} , \tag{1.8}$$

equilibrium requires

$$\frac{\partial g(x, f(x))}{\partial x} = x^{\frac{\gamma}{1 - \gamma}} = -\lambda u'(x) = \lambda(1 - x)^{-1/\sigma} . \tag{1.9}$$

Figure 1.1 shows the three periodic equilibrium points. Shutdown, $x = 0$, is one point. The other two are roots of

$$x^{\frac{\gamma}{1-\gamma}}(1-x)^{1/\sigma} = \lambda . \qquad (1.10)$$

As long as λ is small enough, there are two roots, x_L and x_H.

Let π_L and π_H be the fractions of time spent at the two positive periodic equilibrium points. The labor supply constraint requires

$$\pi_L u(x_L) + \pi_H u(x_H) = u(\bar{x}) . \qquad (1.11)$$

There is a two-dimensional subspace of values of λ, π_L, and π_H that corresponds to three-point periodic equilibria ($x = 0$, x_L, and x_H), three one-dimensional subspaces that correspond to two-point periodic equilibria ($x = 0$ and x_L; $x = 0$ and x_H; $x = x_L$ and x_H), and two isolated points that correspond to unchanging nonperiodic equilibria ($x_L = \bar{x}$ and $x_H = \bar{x}$).

The periodic equilibria with thick-market externalities can be ranked in welfare terms by the average amount of output they produce. The best periodic equilibrium comes closest to the optimal one that maximizes average output by switching

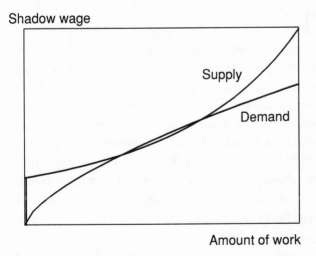

Figure 1.1   *Periodic Equilibrium Points*

back and forth from a low value (zero in the example) to a positive value. Although the optimum may be among the possible periodic equilibria, there is no guarantee that the economy will operate at or near the optimum. Instead, the economy can be in equilibrium in any of its periodic equilibria. If an inefficient cycle becomes established, it is self-replicating. In the framework developed here, all periodic equilibria have equally burdensome work schedules—workers are indifferent among them. But the superior equilibria produce more average output because they take better advantage of the economies of batch production, given increasing returns.

Thick-Market Economies Internal to the Firm

Thick-market economies need not be external to the firm. Indeed, in the spirit of Coase (1937), the firm may extend to the point where at least the more important thick-market economies are within its boundaries. Simple increasing returns in the variable factors of production are one example of a thick-market economy.

A model similar to the one developed earlier in this section illustrates the optimal time schedule of activity in a firm with a dedicated group of workers. The firm maximizes its average level of output subject to a constraint on the utility achieved by the typical worker. Equivalently, it maximizes workers' utility subject to a constraint on average output. The exercise is similar to cost minimization. No explicit assumption is made about the firm's output market, but implicitly the problem is reasonable only if the concavity of the firm's revenue function more than offsets the increasing returns of its technology. Absent this condition, there would be no bound on the size of the firm's work force.

In order to get temporal agglomeration within the firm, it is necessary that the firm operate in a region of increasing returns in those factors that can be varied. If capital services are costless once capital is in place (depreciation occurs over time but not in proportion to use), this condition is stronger than increasing returns in all factors including capital. If the entire cost of capital is incurred *ex post* (only odometer readings matter), then I am assuming increasing returns in the standard sense.

Figure 1.2 shows the utility-production frontier for the firm and its workers. The solid line maps $(u(x),f(x))$ for x between 0 and 1; at $x = 1$, all available hours are devoted to work. For x between x_L and x_H, increasing returns in the technology, thanks to the thick-market effect, dominate the concavity of $u(x)$. If work is always at the level $\bar{x}$, the utility constraint is achieved, but output is only $f(\bar{x})$. With temporal agglomeration, on the other hand, the average level of output can be $y^* > f(\bar{x})$, by working the amount x_L during rest periods and the amount x_H during work spurts.

A special case of figure 1.2 applies to Rogerson's (1988)

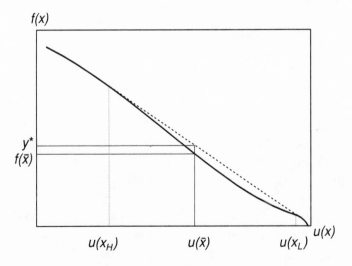

Figure 1.2   Utility-Production Frontier

analysis of fixed costs of work. When the nonconvexity has the form Rogerson assumes, x_L must be zero; the worker conserves on fixed costs of getting to work by taking entire days off. Hence Rogerson's model explains weekends and holidays; the firm and its workers achieve a superior combination of goods production and leisure by concentrating work in 235 workdays out of the 365 available over the year.

Applications of Agglomeration Theory

The analysis of this section—either based on externalities or thick-market effects internal to the firm—has numerous geographical and temporal applications. Some examples are:

LOW	HIGH
Rural areas	Cities
Lobbies	Offices
Night	Day
Weekends	Weekdays
Winter	Summer
Slump	Boom
Weak decade	Strong decade

2. THICK-MARKET ECONOMIES

Peter Diamond (1982) has developed the most thorough and rigorous analysis of a thick-market externality. In his model, the number of customers in the market determines each firm's inventory holding costs. In a thick-market equilibrium, production is high, so there are many customers (no producer consumes its own output). Costs of production and sales are low because the rapid arrival rate of customers means that inventories turn over frequently. Consequently high production levels are profitable. Another equilibrium with a thin market can also occur. Only the superior production opportunities are profitable because inventories turn over slowly.

Diamond's analysis is simpler than the one in the preceding section in one crucial respect: there is no variable factor to be allocated across time periods. The essential idea in section 1 is that the economy can take advantage of a mild thick-market effect by concentrating labor input in one time or place. Because the concentration of the variable input does not occur in Diamond's model, he needs a much stronger thick-market effect to get the result he seeks.

The other important difference is in the nature of the result. In Diamond's model, equation 1.2, without x, is

$$Y_t = g(Y_t) \qquad (2.1)$$

and it has at least two roots. That is, the thick-market externality is so strong that there is a region where the elasticity of $g(\cdot)$ exceeds 1; this property is an implication of Diamond's stochastic search model, not just an assumption. By contrast, I assume only that $g(x, Y)$ has a region of increasing returns in x and Y together, which is consistent with only a mild thick-market effect. Diamond stresses the multiplicity of roots of equation 2.1, whereas I make the assumption that equation 1.2 has only one root or, if there are multiple roots, that the economy chooses the largest one. It is important to note that the pattern of alternation between high and low levels of activity described in the previous section is *not* a movement between the two equilibria described by Diamond. Each is a high-level equilibrium in Diamond's sense. They differ because of different levels of labor input.

Other Sources of Thick-Market Effects

My discussion of thick-market effects at a practical level will deliberately blur the spatial-temporal distinction. I believe that it is useful to consider why activities in big cities might have lower costs in order to understand why activities in booms might have lower costs.

The inventory holding costs characterized very sharply in Diamond's model take many forms in real life. Inventory turnover rates probably differ by more than an order of magnitude between retailers in big cities and small towns. The magnitude of the corresponding holding costs varies widely. It always includes interest and storage costs and may include depreciation for semidurables and obsolescence for style and technological goods.

Selling and buying costs are lower in thick markets. A high density of buyers makes possible higher utilization of salespeople and facilities and permits greater specialization. Compare the efficiency of 47th Street Photo to a camera store in a medium-sized city and to the camera department in a store in a small town. The efficiency probably varies over more than an order of magnitude.

On the buying side, high specialization of sellers and salespeople and lower search and transportation costs mean greater efficiency in purchasing intermediate inputs in thick markets. For established purchasing relationships, thicker markets mean lower transportation costs. For example, in large cities, restaurants rent their knives from a service that delivers sharpened knives every few days. Such a service is much cheaper when the density of restaurants is high. Similarly, the pronounced increase in the use of overnight delivery services in the past decade has made these services much cheaper because customer density is so much greater.

Although the most obvious thick-market economies apply to selling, buying, and distributing goods and services, the economies extend to actual production as well. In thick markets, components are available in much greater variety. Firms in remote locations or in undeveloped countries make parts that are available in the open market in locations with concentrated economic activity. Thick markets offer much more specialized workers and services. Firms outside of urban areas must make do with general practitioners for accounting, consulting, and legal services, or they must incur substantial travel costs to bring in specialists. Perhaps most important, workers and facilities in thick markets achieve higher utilization rates. Compare the number of sandwiches made per day by each worker in a big-city delicatessen to the output of similar workers in small towns.

Finally, a significant element of total cost in businesses arises from collecting and paying bills and from similar activities. In thick markets, workers are more specialized and are in closer contact with their counterparts in other firms.

3. APPLICATION OF TEMPORAL AGGLOMERATION THEORY

Temporal agglomeration can occur whenever thick-market economies overcome the concavity of preferences. Both geographical and temporal agglomeration tend to occur at places or times favored by technology or preferences. Activity concentrates at natural ports, for example. Similarly, the extreme concentration of activity from 9:00 to 12:00 in the morning and from 1:00 to 5:00 in the afternoon reflects humankind's diurnal pattern of attentiveness. * On the other hand, the timing of weekends (but not the length of the week) is completely arbitrary.

The seasonal pattern of economic activity presents a particularly interesting example of temporal agglomeration. Al-

---

* Of course, there is the deeper question of why humans are diurnal. In particular, neurophysiologists consider most mammals' need to sleep quite a few hours a day an unsolved mystery. Temporal agglomeration may be the answer—the concentration of activity in daylight hours and the complete suppression of physical activity during sleep may have an evolutionary advantage.

though the third quarter (July, August, and September) is the time most favored for vacations in the United States, that quarter has the highest level of labor input over the entire year (Barsky and Miron 1988). The third-quarter peak in production is strong in many industries besides food processing and construction, where the role of weather is obvious.

The annual boom in the sale of durable goods at Christmas is an excellent example of temporal agglomeration at work. In any economy without thick-market economies and other features conducive to agglomeration, the Christmas boom would have to be explained by a strong preference on the part of most families to shop in December, even though the prices of goods would be higher and the shopper would do better to buy earlier in the year or just after Christmas. In fact, the Christmas boom has a very different character. First, consumers gain by concentrating their annual shopping for some kinds of goods into a six-week period. A long shopping list makes each visit to a store more productive. They also gain because the selection of products is wider than at other times of the year. Second, the selling process is much more productive during the Christmas boom, with inventories turning over faster than at other times of the year. Sales per salesperson and per square foot are substantially higher. One of the confirmations that thick-market economies are at work is that there is no systematic tendency toward higher prices during the Christmas boom (Barsky, Kimball, and Warner 1988).

The most interesting application of temporal agglomeration theory in macroeconomics is to booms and recessions. Is it reasonable to consider a several-year boom to be a cousin of the Christmas boom? Is a recession similar to the January contraction? An important difference between macroeconomic expansions and contractions, on the one hand, and diurnal, weekly, and seasonal movements, on the other, is the unpredictability of the former. Seasonal fluctuations occur in precise synchrony with the earth's revolution around the sun, but the business cycle is not in obvious synchrony with any single outside driving force. The only general statements that seem to hold for the U.S. economy are that a rise in interest rates often precedes a recession and that movements in GNP are correlated with movements in government purchases in goods and services. Not only is the business cycle irregular within any single country, but the intensity of the cycle varies across countries. Some countries, notably France, have almost no fluctuations in output or employment over two- to ten-year periods, even though daily, weekly, and annual cycles are similar to other developed economies of the northern hemisphere.

Still, many of the same elements that make thick-market effects a plausible explanation of sharp seasonal fluctuations seem to apply to the business cycle as well. Just as New York is a good place to go shopping even though its stores sell a greater volume per square foot than those in other less congested cities and towns, a boom is a good time for consumers to buy. And the efficiencies in buying, producing, distributing, and selling that offset the convexity of technology and preferences should apply just as much to the random fluctuations of the business cycle as to the systematic fluctuations by season.

I think temporal agglomeration theory has a number of applications to business cycles. First, the optimal pattern of activity over time may be in synchrony with cyclical driving forces, such as government purchases. Second, the inefficient temporal pattern associated with thick-market externalities may also be in synchrony with irregular driving forces. Third, a boom or slump may represent the shift of the economy from one periodic equilibrium to another, as a result of some impulse.

Rogerson (1988) and, following Rogerson's suggestion, Prescott (1986) are the leading proponents of theories in which the business cycle represents efficient temporal agglomeration. Figure 1.3, which repeats the gist of figure 1.2, is helpful

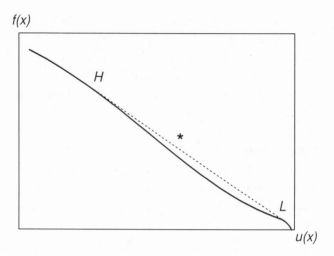

Figure 1.3   Utility-Production Frontier

in understanding Rogerson's idea. By construction, points H and L are equivalent. First, they provide the double root $Y_H = g(x_H, Y_H)$ and $Y_L = g(x_L, Y_L)$. Second, H and L are points of indifference in the following sense: the extra output produced during a brief spell at H is just enough to compensate the worker for the foregone leisure, relative to L.

Optimality requires dividing time between H and L so as to achieve the point ∗. There may not be an exact prescription, however, for the time pattern of the alternation—the only strong prescription is that the long-run average be at ∗. Hence a variable pattern, such as a random business cycle, that achieves ∗ as an average may involve little or no social cost relative to a stable daily, weekly, and annual schedule. When there is some cyclical driving force, such as changes in government purchases or in productivity, the pattern of temporal agglomeration will synchronize with the driving force. This is Rogerson's and Prescott's basic point.

Whereas the predictable pattern of daily, weekly, and annual movements between active and resting states of the economy synchronizes with the clock and the calendar, the business cycle synchronizes with random events. Wartime, with large increases in government purchases, invariably activates the economy. Financial crises are usually followed by recession and higher incidence of inactive periods. Fluctuations in the work schedules of individual workers take the form of variations in annual weeks of work more than variations in hours per day.

The cyclical mechanism sketched here amplifies small disturbances. For example, a small increase in consumption will activate the economy, making it a more desirable time to consume (just as December is the best time to buy durables). In Prescott's real business cycle model, temporal agglomeration in the particular form proposed by Rogerson makes the economy activate itself when there is a favorable shift of technology.

In the real business cycle model, the synchrony of economic activity with a driving force is efficient, because the thick-market effect is internal to the firm and its workers. When a thick-market externality causes the economy to cycle through a periodic equilibrium, there is no presumption of efficiency. By extension, there is no presumption of efficiency if a periodic equilibrium synchronizes with a driving force. In that case, so-called booms are periods in which the economy spends a longer time than usual in the most active state. Later slack times enable the economy to satisfy the long-run requirement about the fraction of time in each periodic state.

A related idea is that a boom is a time when the economy shifts from one periodic equilibrium to another. Figure 1.4 illustrates how this works. The tricky part is to explain why employment as well as output rises in a boom. The curving band contains the average level of employment and the average level of output for each periodic equilibrium. All of the equilibria assign work schedules with the same level of utility. Schedules with low variability have higher average levels of

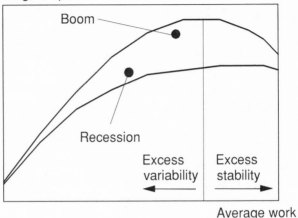

Figure 1.4   Output and Employment Variability

employment; schedules with high variability have low average employment. To achieve the same level of satisfaction, workers require compensation in the form of higher leisure in order to accept the disamenity of higher variability.

In the U.S. economy, employment and output move together. Hence, if the cycle involves movements from one periodic equilibrium to another, the leading case would be movements along the curve to the left of the optimum, which slopes upward. There, the economy always has too much instability in employment. A boom occurs when employment becomes more stable, which increases output. In a boom workers give up leisure without sacrificing satisfaction from their work schedules. Although their total leisure is reduced, it is better timed.

The width of the band in figure 1.4 depends on the extent to which the third and additional periodic equilibrium points create the possibility of work schedules with the same variability as the optimal schedules, but less output because the extra points are poorly placed. If the band is sufficiently wide, there is another story about booms and recessions—a boom occurs when the economy moves northeast in the diagram. In a boom work schedules are rationalized, producing more output with less variability.

The temporal agglomeration view of the business cycle does not imply optimality of particular cyclical episodes, nor does it suggest that every episode of depressed economic activity is just a normal lull between episodes of concentrated output. In particular, I make no suggestion that the Great Depression was an extended rest. On the contrary, I think agglomeration theory makes an important contribution to the type of story told by Bernanke (1983): the Depression was the result of a severe injury to the networks that make high levels of output possible. Recent thought has singled out the financial system—the network that provides credit and executes transactions. Other networks are essential as well. What would happen to the GNP of the United States if the telephone system shut down for an extended period?

4. EMPIRICAL IMPLICATIONS OF TEMPORAL AGGLOMERATION

Most modern economies have volatile output and stable relative prices. Prices are not the shock absorbers described by neoclassical economics. This observation has led some macroeconomists to posit price rigidity as a starting point for theory. Temporal agglomeration theory derives output volatility from assumptions about technology and preferences. What about the stability of relative prices?

With respect to the real wage, figure 1.1 shows that the shadow wage moves in tandem with employment in a periodic equilibrium with a thick-market externality. The same analysis applies to optimal time agglomeration as well. There are several reasons why measured wages might be stable in spite of figure 1.1. First, wages may smooth the shadow wage over the periodic cycle—the wage paid at any given point may not be the allocative shadow wage. The same consideration applies to any macroeconomic model. Second, the labor supply schedule may fluctuate from one periodic equilibrium point to the next. Labor supply is greater during the day than at night, for example. Although supply shifts are not likely to be important for the business cycle, they could be important over the seasons. Third, the labor supply schedule may be highly elastic—again, this consideration stabilizes real wages in any macroeconomic model. Fourth, and most interesting and important, thick-market externalities may accrue directly to workers. If some of the benefits of thick markets take the form of higher take-home pay in relation to wages paid, or greater job satisfaction, the shadow value of work will be higher during periods of high activity even if wages paid by employers remain the same. Akerlof, Rose, and Yellen (1988) argue that low-unemployment markets generate substantial improvements in job satisfaction because workers are better able to move to more satisfying jobs when the market is fluid. They demonstrate the importance of voluntary job changes that do not raise cash wages.

For established, long-term workers, wage smoothing is probably the most important element of the explanation of constant real wages. For mobile workers, lower job-search cost and faster job finding in thicker markets may be the most important element in the explanation of stable real wages. Wider selection of jobs with better matching and higher job satisfaction may also be significant.

The seasonal and cyclical stability of relative goods prices may be explained by considerations similar to those for real wages. Temporal agglomeration may be more pronounced for durable goods than for nondurables, for example. In the simplest model, the relative price of durables would fall along with the output of durables. But, just as with the real wage, there may be synchronization of the periodic cycle with shifts in preferences. For example, the Christmas boom in durables is the result of the suitability of these goods as presents. Second, it seems clear that the customers share in thick-market benefits. As I mentioned in section 2, thick markets have wider selections and lower shopping costs. Seasonal and cyclical booms are times of lower shadow values of durables even if the relative price of durables is stable, because of the rise in consumer benefits not reflected in the price.

The intertemporal relative price of goods—the real interest rate—also obeys the principles just laid out. In the simplest model, the interest rate governing the deferral of the use of goods from the low state to the high state should be higher than the one from high to low. Over the year the interest rate from March to September should be high and the rate from September to March should be low. In fact, there are almost no seasonal variations in real interest rates. As in the previous cases, movements in preferences and thick-market benefits accruing directly to consumers could explain the stability of real rates.

Productivity

The two sources of temporal agglomeration considered here—thick-market externalities and increasing returns from internal thick-market economies or other sources—both reveal themselves in productivity calculations. When some exogenous force stimulates output, measured productivity rises (Hall 1988a, 1988b).

In the case of a thick-market externality, the production function is

$$Y = g(x, Y) . \qquad (4.1)$$

Solow's total factor productivity calculation starts with the finite difference approximation,

$$\Delta Y \doteq \frac{\partial g}{\partial x} \Delta x + \frac{\partial g}{\partial Y} \Delta Y. \tag{4.2}$$

Under competition, the marginal product of labor is equated to the real wage,

$$\frac{\partial g}{\partial x} = \frac{w}{p}. \tag{4.3}$$

Because $Y = g(x, Y)$, the marginal externality, $\partial g / \partial Y$, can be written as an elasticity, $(Y/g)\partial g / \partial Y$. Call this elasticity $\gamma/(1 + \gamma)$. Then

$$\frac{\Delta Y}{Y} \doteq \frac{wx}{pY} \frac{\Delta x}{x} + \frac{\gamma}{1 + \gamma} \frac{\Delta Y}{Y}, \tag{4.4}$$

or

$$\frac{\Delta Y}{Y} \doteq (1 + \gamma) \frac{wx}{pY} \frac{\Delta x}{x}. \tag{4.5}$$

Solow's calculation assumes no externality ($\gamma = 0$). Consequently, it gives too little weight to the change in labor input, $\Delta x/x$, and the calculation of the productivity residual,

$$\frac{\Delta Y}{Y} - \frac{wx}{pY} \frac{\Delta x}{x}, \tag{4.6}$$

records an increase in productivity any time some force causes an increase in employment.

For increasing returns, resulting from thick-market economies or other sources, the production function is

$$Y = f(x). \tag{4.7}$$

Again taking finite differences, I get

$$\Delta Y \doteq f'(x) \Delta x. \tag{4.8}$$

Let $1 + \gamma$ be the elasticity of $f(x)$ with respect to x. Then

$$\frac{\Delta Y}{Y} \doteq (1 + \gamma) \frac{\Delta x}{x}. \qquad (4.9)$$

The Solow residual, calculated as in formula 4.6, will record false productivity growth when employment rises because of the omission of the γ. The effect will be worsened if labor's share, wx/pY, is less than one.

5. CONCLUSIONS

Temporal agglomeration provides a workable theoretical framework for understanding the volatility of output, the stability of relative prices, and the correlation of output and productivity growth. Existing general equilibrium models fall short of satisfactory explanations of these phenomena. The neoclassical model predicts smooth evolution of activity over time; it cannot explain the concentration of activity over the day, the week, the year, or the business cycle. Temporal agglomeration makes endogenous the shifts in productivity that the real business cycle model invokes as an exogenous driving force.

TWO

Measuring Noise

The output of goods and services of the business sector of the U.S. economy displays considerable volatility. Understanding this volatility is one of the central concerns of macroeconomics. In this chapter I consider the following basic question: Are the fluctuations in output primarily a response to changes in the volume of goods and services delivered to users outside the business sector (consumers, government, or foreigners), or do the fluctuations arise spontaneously within the sector? The research demonstrates a substantial spontaneous element of output. In particular, much of the variability of output from one year to the next is unrelated to changes in deliveries of goods and services to users. Yet much of the lower-frequency movement of output is associated with changes in the volume of goods delivered to outside users.

By definition, goods produced by the business sector but not delivered to outside users constitute investment. Because this research considers output conditional on deliveries, it is as much about the volatility of investment as it is about the volatility of production. And it is no surprise to any student of the aggregate U.S. economy that investment, especially inventory investment, is volatile. The literature on inventory investment has noted many times that contractions in that component of investment alone are often about as large as the contractions in total GNP at the outsets of recessions. What is novel here is a full consideration of the extent to which the movements of investment are induced by actual or expected changes in deliveries. The model gives a full rational-expectations treatment to the accelerator. Interestingly, it finds that a large part of the cyclical movements of inventory investment are induced by changes in deliveries. The spontaneous element of investment comes mainly, but not exclusively, from fixed investment.

1. THE BASIC APPROACH TO MEASURING THE SPONTANEOUS ELEMENT OF OUTPUT

Consider an economy whose business sector delivers goods and services in volume z_t. The variable z_t is not exogenous in any sense; rather, I simply consider the problem of scheduling output conditional on z_t. The business sector produces output y_t. Any output not shipped is accumulated as capital, k_t, with survival rate δ, so the capital stock evolves according to

$$k_t = y_t - z_t + \delta k_{t-1} . \qquad (1.1)$$

The technology is most efficient when there are ψ units of capital for each unit of output produced; the cost function is

$$\frac{1}{2} \sum (k_t - \psi y_{t+1})^2 . \qquad (1.2)$$

Note that capital is measured at the end of the period and the capital must be in place in advance in order for production to take place.

Let

$$\omega = \frac{\psi}{1 + \psi\delta} < 1 . \qquad (1.3)$$

The solution to the problem of minimizing expected cost is

$$k_t^e = \omega k_{t-1} + \omega E_t \sum_{i=0}^{\infty} \omega^i(z_{t+i+1} - \omega z_{t+i}) . \qquad (1.4)$$

That is, capital is a weighted average of future expected sales. The ^{e} indicates that this is the theoretical value for output without noise. Actual capital is its theoretical values plus noise:

$$k_t = k_t^e + s_t . \qquad (1.5)$$

Following an insight of LeRoy-Porter (1981) and Shiller (1981), I will find it useful to introduce the "perfect foresight" variable,

$$k_t^* = \omega k_{t-1} + \omega \sum_{i=0}^{\infty} \omega^i(z_{t+i+1} - \omega z_{t+i}) . \qquad (1.6)$$

The $*$ variables are observable by the econometrician long after the fact. Let $\epsilon_{t,i}$ be the difference between actual sales at time $t + i$ and sales expected at time $t + i$ as of time t. Then the observable discrepancy between the actual and the $*$ versions of the variables can be expressed as

$$k_t - k_t^* = s_t - \omega \sum_{i=0}^{\infty} \omega^i(\varepsilon_{t,\,i+1} - \omega\epsilon_{t,\,i})$$

$$= s_t - v_t . \qquad (1.7)$$

That is, the discrepancy between the actual capital stock and the perfect foresight value is noise less a composite expectation error, v_t. The expectation error obeys the standard orthogonality condition of rational expectations:

$$E\,(v_t|x_t) = 0 \qquad (1.8)$$

---

where x_t is any vector of data known to the firm when the investment decision is taken. Note that the composite expectation error, v_t, is serially correlated, but the correlation does not involve a failure of the orthogonality condition because lagged values of v are not in the information set; v_t is not observed until long after time t.

To obtain information about the noise, I make use of the technique developed in Durlauf and Hall (1988). Let M_x be the projection operator onto current and lagged value of x_t; for a time series u_t, $M_x u_t$ is the fitted values of the regression of u_t on $x_t, x_{t-1}, \ldots$. Then the projection of the discrepancy in x yields information about noise:

$$(k_t - k_t^*)M_x = M_x v_t + M_x s_t . \tag{1.9}$$

The firm term, $M_x v_t$, is zero by rational expectations. Regressing the discrepancy on the x-variables eliminates the expectation error. The remainder,

$$\hat{s}_t = M_x s_t , \tag{1.10}$$

is a conservative estimate of the noise in the following sense: the variance of $\hat{s}_t$ is less than the variance of noise, s_t. The reason is simple. The noise variable can be decomposed into the fitted value, $\hat{s}_t$, plus an orthogonal residual:

$$s_t = \hat{s}_t + u_t , \tag{1.11}$$

so

$$V(s_t) = V(\hat{s}_t) + V(u_t) \tag{1.12}$$

and

$$V(s_t) \geq V(\hat{s}_t) . \tag{1.13}$$

The procedure I shall use to make inferences about the spontaneous element of investment is the following. First, I shall form the discrepancy between actual capital and the amount of capital mandated by the model under perfect foresight. The discrepancy arises because of expectation errors and because of the spontaneous element. Then I shall regress the discrepancy on well-chosen variables known to firms when investment decisions are taken. The test for the existence of noise is simply whether any of the variables have nonzero coefficients in the regression. Finally, the fitted value from the regression is a conservative estimate of the noise time series.

2. FIXED CAPITAL AND INVENTORIES

It is important to extend the model by distinguishing two major components of the capital stock—fixed capital and inventories. Investment in fixed capital involves a lag of a year or more for planning and installation. Inventories respond almost immediately to changes in the economy. I denote the stock of inventories as v_t and extend the cost function as

$$\frac{1}{2} \sum \gamma^t [(k_t - \psi y_{t+1})^2 + \alpha(v_t - \phi y_{t+1})^2]. \qquad (2.14)$$

Here $\gamma < 1$ is the discount ratio and α is the relative weight of inventory discrepancies. Let τ be the time to build fixed capital. At time $t - \tau$ the firm makes its plan for capital to be in place in period t. This decision is conditional on the amount of fixed capital already committed to be in place in period $t - 1$ and on the level of inventories expected at the end of period $t - 1$:

$$k_t^* = \omega^k k_{t-1} + E_{t-\tau} \left[\omega^v v_{t-1} + \sum_{i=0}^{\infty} \omega_i z_{t+i} \right]. \qquad (2.15)$$

Then at time t, the firm makes its plan for inventories to be in place at the end of period t. The capital stock for periods t, $t + 1, \ldots, t + \tau - 1$ is given, so the plan is conditional on the known values of $k_{t-1}, \ldots, k_{t+\tau-1}$ and v_{t-1}. Thus

32

$$v_t^* = \sum_{j=0}^{\tau} \beta_j^k \, k_{t-j-1} + \beta^v \, v_{t-1} - E_{t-\tau} \sum_{i=0}^{\infty} \beta_i z_{t+i} \, . \qquad (2.16)$$

Calculation of the coefficients in these formulas follows standard principles for quadratic optimization.

The information available at time $t - \tau$ relevant to the determination of k_t includes all variables known at the beginning of period $t - \tau$ plus the committed values of the capital stock through period t. If candidate x-variables are time averages through the period, then the latest admissible variables are those observed during period $t - \tau - 1$. In addition, the capital stock through period $t - 1$ is admissible. If the assumption implicit in the cost function is literally true—that cost depends only on the end-of-period stocks—then variables dated t would be admissible as well. If the discrete-time problem, however, is really an approximation to a continuous-time problem, then the variables dated t are not admissible. In this work, I do not use the contemporaneous variables.

For the inventory equation, I use variables dated $t - 1$ and earlier.

Estimation

I will use the value of 0.9 for the discount ratio, γ, and 0.9 for the capital survival rate, δ. For the parameters ψ and ϕ, I use the sample averages of the fixed capital/output ratio and the inventory/output ratio; these values are 1.32 and 0.245. The only econometric slope parameter I estimate is the relative cost of inventory discrepancies, α. To estimate this parameter, I note that the difference between the first-order condition for fixed capital, k_t, and the one for inventories, v_t, is

$$k_t - \psi y_t = \alpha \frac{1 - \psi(1 - \delta)}{1 + \phi(1 - \delta)}(v_t - \phi y_t). \qquad (2.17)$$

According to the model, this relation is deterministic. Of course, in practice, there is a random disturbance in the relation. It is not very large, however, in comparison to the movements in the variables. Under an errors-in-variables interpretation, with errors uncorrelated with the true values of the variables, the value of α lies between the regression estimate of equation 2.17 and the estimate obtained by reversing left- and right-hand variables and taking the reciprocal of the regression coefficient. Because the fit is quite good, the bound is fairly tight. I used the average of the two estimates.

3. THE DATA

The study uses annual data from the U.S. National Income and Product Accounts (NIPA). The sales of the business sector, z_t, are consumption, government purchases of goods and services less government production, and net exports. Production of the business sector, y_t, consists of sales plus investment (inventory investment and fixed investment). Note that the provision of housing services is considered part of the business sector—one of the sources of spontaneous volatility is fluctuations in construction of new housing. All other consumer durables are treated as deliveries to consumers and do not contribute to business volatility.

Figure 2.1 shows the basic data in detrended form (econometric results are obtained from the original data, not the detrended data). Output always exceeds sales because of the deterioration of capital. Plainly, output is more volatile than sales. The recessions of 1973–75 and 1981–82 stand out as times when production fell dramatically but sales remained roughly constant. The relative volatility of the two series does not answer the question posed here because it fails to account for the accelerator. The accelerator, however, is unable to

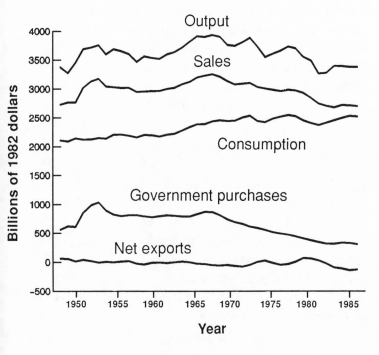

Figure 2.1   Output, Sales, and Components

explain the jagged movements of output, as the results of the next section show.

In the first half of the sample period, changes in military purchases were a major source of volatility in sales. The sharp peak of purchases in 1953 for the Korean War and the smaller peak in 1968 for Vietnam show clearly in total sales. Sales reached a trough around 1960 between the two wars and at a time when consumption was low. Then sales grew rapidly through the 1960s to a peak around 1970. Consumption was the key component in this growth. Starting in the mid-1970s, volatility in net exports became important. Sales have been relatively constant since 1970, but net exports have tended to move in the opposite direction from consumption and government purchases.

It would not be plausible to suggest that sales or components of sales, except government purchases, were exogenous with respect to production. Sales occur in a market that allocates the productive capacity of the business sector. I propose in this section to examine production conditional on sales; there is no hypothesis that sales cause production.

4. RESULTS

The parameters of the model are the capital/output ratio, ψ, the survival rate of capital, δ, the inventory/output ratio, ϕ, the discount ratio, γ, and the relative cost of inventory discrepancies, α. There are robust estimators for ψ and ϕ that do not require econometric estimation of slope coefficients. Take an estimate of the survival rate of capital—I used 90 percent per year. Compute the capital stock from a reasonable initial benchmark and the recursion,

$$k_t = \delta k_{t-1} + i_t , \qquad (4.1)$$

where i_t is gross investment in fixed capital from the national income and product accounts. Then estimate the capital/output ratio, ψ, as the average of the ratio of k_t to y_{t+1}. For ϕ, simply take the average of the ratio of the stock of inventories as reported in the NIPA to production. As I noted earlier, the only slope parameter is α. The estimate of α obtained by treating equation 2.17 as a regression is 3.27 with a standard error of 0.40. The estimate obtained by reversing the variables and taking the reciprocal of the coefficient is 5.58. My estimate of α is the average of the two, 4.72. The results would hardly be affected by different choices of α within this interval; α affects only the short-run adjustment to surprises and not the relation between future sales and current investment.

Figure 2.2 shows the level of output that would have occurred if firms had known the actual path of sales many years

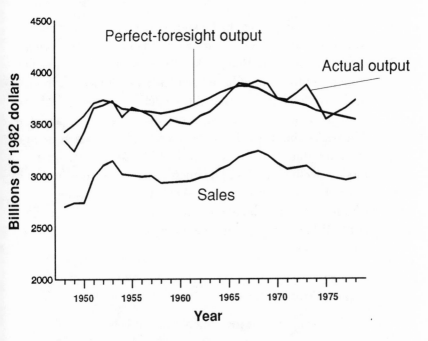

Figure 2.2 Perfect-Foresight Output

in advance. This output series is different from the one implied by the * variables because they are computed year by year with actual capital and inventory stocks, whereas the output series in figure 2.2 does not depend on initial stocks. This output series cannot form the basis of a rigorous noise measurement, but it does give an indication of the overall departures from the path that would have been optimal according to the model with perfect foresight. The departures of actual from predicted output in figure 2.2 are a mixture of expectation errors and model noise.

In figure 2.2, perfect-foresight output, y_t^*, has the same basic low-frequency movements as actual output, and those movements are dictated by similar movements in deliveries, z_t. There are, however, some important differences between perfect-foresight and actual output. In particular, in the early 1960s the business sector would have produced substantially more output than it did had it known that sales would grow so much later in the 1960s. A similar shortfall of output occurred before the Korean War. After 1970, with sales relatively smooth, output would have been fairly smooth as well if the business sector had obeyed the model and enjoyed perfect foresight about sales. Instead, actual output was quite jagged. The peak of output in 1973 was not related to any increase in sales, and the sharp contraction in 1975 came a year after a modest decline in sales. The question to be answered in this research is whether the ups and downs in actual output not warranted by the subsequent movements in deliveries can be attributed to imperfect information or whether they are spontaneous noise.

Noise in Fixed Investment

The level of gross investment mandated by the model is

$$i_t^e = k_t^e - \delta k_{t-1} . \tag{4.2}$$

When gross investment is determined in period $t - \tau$, the amount is sufficient to bring the capital stock for period t up to the optimal level, k_t^e, from its level already committed for the previous period, k_{t-1}. Actual gross investment is

$$i_t = k_t - \delta k_{t-1} . \tag{4.3}$$

Hence noise in investment is

$$i_t - i_t^e = k_t - k_t^e = s_t . \tag{4.4}$$

Even though investment is approximately the first difference of capital, the level of noise in investment is equal to noise in capital. The fitted values for the regression of $k_t - k_t^*$ on the x-variables are estimates of noise in investment.

Figure 2.3 shows $k_t - k_t^*$ for the period 1951 through 1978 (later years are lost in the calculation of k_t^*). The figure also shows the level of gross investment. Both variables are de-

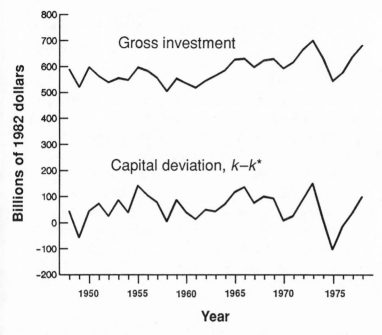

Figure 2.3   Gross Investment and Capital Deviation

trended by the trend of deliveries. Except for the higher level of investment, the two series are very similar. The similarity is paradoxical for the rational expectations accelerator model, according to which the difference between k_t and k_t^* should be an expectation error, uncorrelated with any information available when k_t was chosen.

Under the assumption that the time to build is two years or less, variables dated $t - 3$ or earlier are eligible regressors for detecting noise. In addition, future capital is known over the horizon of the time to build, so values of k dated $t - 1$ and earlier are eligible regressors. The regression using just the lagged values of the actual capital stock is

$$k_t - k_t^* = 33.9 + .87k_{t-1} - 1.69k_{t-2} + .82k_{t-3} \quad (4.5)$$

$$R^2 = .402 \qquad F = 5.37$$

The large coefficients on lagged actual capital show the presence of a large noise component. Because k_{t-1} contains the noise variable, it is the logical candidate to be the most powerful x-variable in the noise-detection regression. I have not been able to find other variables that have unambiguous predictive value for $k_t - k_t^*$ three years in advance, once lagged capital is included in the noise-detection regression.

Figure 2.4 shows the estimated conservative noise series (the fitted values from equation 4.5) in comparison to actual fixed investment. Noise is shown to be a major factor in the overall movements of fixed investment. The rational expectations accelerator model leaves much of the volatility of investment unexplained; the hypothesis that the volatility can be attributed to information limitations is refuted by the regression.

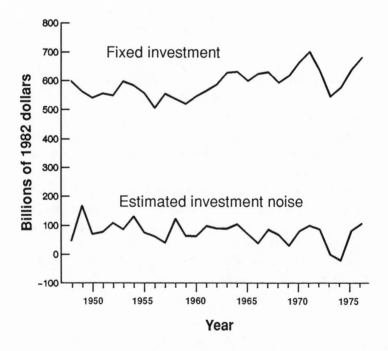

Figure 2.4   Fixed Investment and Investment Noise

Noise in Inventory Investment

Figure 2.5 shows $v_t - v_t^*$ in relation to actual inventory investment. The calculation of perfect-foresight inventories, v_t^*, takes the actual level of capital as given for years t and $t + 1$ because of a two-year time to build for fixed capital; this restriction has a large effect on the coefficients relating inventory investment to its determinants but little effect on the actual values of $v_t - v_t^*$. Again, movements in the difference, $v_t - v_t^*$, are strongly correlated at business-cycle frequencies. This correlation is paradoxical within a model where the difference arises purely from an expectation error. In addition, there is a rise in $v_t - v_t^*$ in the late 1960s. During the remaining years of the sample, the actual level of inventories is chronically well above the level mandated by the model. The model does not

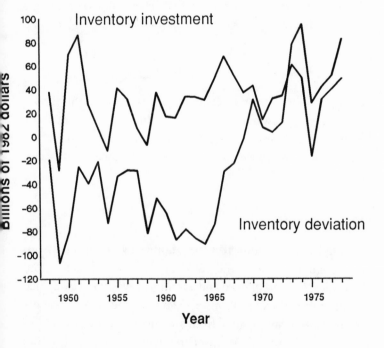

Figure 2.5   Inventory Investment and Inventory Deviation

account for the permanent rise in the inventory/production ratio that occurred in the late 1960s. Instead, it asks that there be inventory disinvestment each year because it finds that the level of inventories coming into the year is excessive by the standards of the model. As a result, there is much more noise in calculations that take the inventory stock of the previous year as given than there is in the calculations underlying Figure 2.2 where the previous inventory level is taken to be that mandated by the model instead of the actual level.

I assume that there is no important time to build inventories, at least in an annual model. Therefore all variables dated $t - 1$ and earlier are eligible as noise-detecting regressors. The variables I use are a time trend (to deal with the trend in the inventory / production ratio), lagged inventories, and a financial variable. The latter is the spread between the six-month commercial paper rate and the three-month Treasury bill rate, an indicator of financial stress that has been shown to be a good predictor of recessions. The noise-detecting regression is

$$v_t - v_t^* = -89 - 8.0t + .65v_{t-1} - 16.1R_{t-1} \qquad (4.6)$$
$$R^2 = .860 \; F = 49.25 \; .$$

Figure 2.6 shows the conservative noise series from this regression, in comparison to inventory investment. Again, the bulk of the movements in inventory investment come from sources other than those considered in the rational-expectations accelerator model.

Noise in Output

Figure 2.7 summarizes the findings on the spontaneous element of investment and output. It decomposes total output into sales, the part of fixed and inventory investment explained by the rational expectations accelerator, and noise. The explained part is simply total fixed and inventory investment less the two noise series. At lower frequencies, sales and output

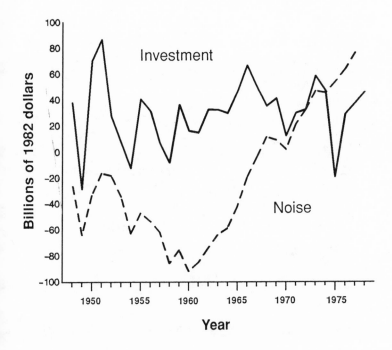

Figure 2.6   Inventory Investment and Inventory Noise

move together with amplitudes greater than either part of investment. At higher frequencies, noise is somewhat larger than the accelerator part of investment. In a number of fluctuations, noise was a dominant part of the story.

The noise series in figure 2.7 is conservative. Only the part of the noise that can be associated with variables observed at least a year earlier is included. Any other elements of noise are included in the rational expectations accelerator term. Unless movements of noise are found to be correlated with some observed variable, there is no way to refute the hypothesis that they are expectation errors; there is no content to the concept of an expectation error apart from lack of correlation with variables known at the time the expectation is formed.

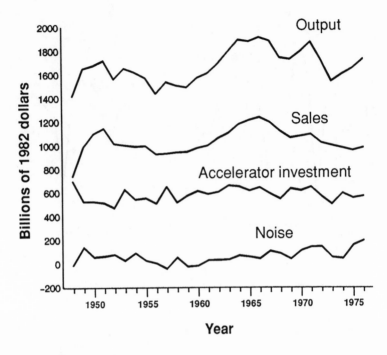

Figure 2.7 Output and Its Components

5. CONCLUSIONS

Output is substantially more volatile than it would be if the timing of sales were the same but the business sector scheduled production to minimize deviations from the prescribed capital-output ratio. Noise detection regressions show clearly that there is a large element of investment and hence output that cannot be explained by the rational-expectations accelerator model.

Factor substitution and financial responses are potentially important influences omitted from the accelerator model, which are therefore included in measured noise. The finding that inventory investment noise is associated with the spread between commercial paper and Treasury bills is one indication that a period of financial stress causes an inventory sell-off that is not contemplated by the accelerator model.

THREE

General Equilibrium with Noise

Construction of general equi-
librium models of the volatility of output and employment has
been dominated by the real business cycle models in the past
few years. The prototypical real business cycle model posits a
source of noise, usually vibrations in the production function,
and a propagation mechanism, usually high elasticity of labor
supply. As Prescott (1986) has shown, such a model is capable
of explaining the observed volatility of output. By invoking a
sufficiently high elasticity of labor supply, he shows that the
observed fluctuations in productivity are big enough to stimulate fluctuations in employment and output of realistic magnitude. Vibrations of the production function are not the only
driving force; other types of noise, such as shifts in preferences,
can help explain the volatility of output within fairly simple
aggregate models.

Though the recent upsurge of interest in real business
cycle models has called attention to the importance of real
sources of fluctuations, monetary nonneutrality and the corresponding importance of monetary sources of fluctuations
remain a central topic in macroeconomics. Research on
monetary nonneutrality has had two branches. One, best
represented by Robert Lucas's (1972) celebrated model of

limited information, derives nonneutral outcomes by making highly specific assumptions within an economic model based on otherwise standard principles. The outcome can properly be described as a full economic equilibrium; within the specified restrictions, there are no unexploited opportunities for trade. Interestingly, although Lucas's paper is among the major landmarks of recent macroeconomics, there has been relatively little additional work on monetary nonneutrality in the equilibrium mode. Equilibrium analysis has become increasingly popular, but almost always "without some features of the payment and credit technologies," in Edward Prescott's (1986) words.

The second branch starts from the observation that prices appear to be unresponsive to monetary developments in the short run. Whereas models along the lines of Lucas's derive the unresponsiveness as a feature of general equilibrium, work in the second branch portrays rigidity as rational behavior at the level of the firm. A huge literature, starting from the Phelps volume (1970), has sought to rationalize the following model: sellers of products or labor services enter into call-option contracts with buyers. The contracts predetermine a price in terms of money. Later, when information about demand becomes available, the buyer chooses the quantity. Plainly, such contracts create monetary nonneutralities during the period when money prices are predetermined. The question addressed by the research is why rational parties would enter into such contracts.

My purpose is to set up a simple general framework for thinking about both real and monetary sources of output volatility. The goal is to be sufficiently general to encompass real business cycle models and models with monetary nonneutrality in both the Lucas and option-contract styles. The framework I develop attempts to push the textbook aggregate demand–aggregate supply (AD-AS) apparatus to the next stage of analytical development. The most important modification is to relax a very strong assumption of the AD-AS model, that product supply is completely inelastic with respect to all relative prices. Because high elasticity of supply is at the heart of the real business cycle view, there is a fundamental disagreement between the AD-AS model and that view. The elasticity of supply is, of course, an empirical issue, and the AD-AS model is vigorously defended by its proponents as making a realistic assumption that the elasticity is low.

The general model developed here is a simple equilibrium model with two markets—one for produced goods and one for the monetary instruments of the government. Product supply, product demand, and money demand all may contain monetary nonneutralities. In the model, a nonneutrality appears simply as the presence of the money price of goods in the supply and demand functions for goods and its presence with an elasticity different from one in the demand function for money. The model does not commit itself to any particular theory of nonneutrality—that property could arise from misperceptions or from precommitments to nominal payments. In the latter case, the real effects of nominal precommitments could result from option contracts as in the standard model of price rigidity or from the distributional effects of efficient nominal contracts.

One of the clearest ways to see the generalization of the AD-AS model achieved here is to consider the impact of an exogenous rise in product demand on the price level. In the AD-AS model, such a rise shifts AD to the right and leaves AS unchanged. The price level rises. In an equilibrium model with monetary neutrality, however, the price level falls, because output rises and the money stock remains the same. In the general model developed here, the impact of an increase in product demand on the price level is ambiguous. If product supply is inelastic, then the price level rises. But if product supply is somewhat elastic, an exogenous increase in product demand will raise equilibrium output and may result in a lower, not a higher, price level.

1. THE MODEL

The model deals with three jointly determined variables: output, y, the price level, p, and a relative price, r, which may be the real interest rate or related intertemporal relative price, the real wage, or the relative price of two kinds of output. The government sets the quantity of its monetary liabilities, M, exogenously. The model is set forth first in general terms; a completely specific example with preferences and technology described in detail will follow. The demand and supply functions have the usual form and interpretation for a general equilibrium model—they characterize the choices made by price-taking actors who can buy and sell the quantities they choose, given preferences, technology, and existing contracts. Throughout the discussion, I shall make the simplifying assumption that the government pays interest on money at a rate equal to the market nominal interest rate less a constant. This assumption rules out the type of nonneutrality considered by Tobin (1965). It also makes it possible to give a sharp definition of monetary nonneutrality in terms of the presence of the price level in the supply or demand functions. Because the service price of money is always equal to the constant chosen by the government, it need not appear explicitly in the model.

The product demand schedule is

$$y = D(r,p) . \qquad (1.1)$$

Demand arises from consumption, investment, and government purchases. If demand depends on the money price level, p, there is a nonneutrality in demand. For example, if nominal contracts have the effect of redistributing income from actors who tend to hold physical wealth to those who tend to hold financial wealth when the money price level changes, p will appear in the demand function.

The product supply schedule is

$$y = S(r,p) . \tag{1.2}$$

Because the labor market does not appear explicitly, S characterizes choices about the amount of work as well as the technology. Again, p enters if there are nonneutralities. These could arise, for example, from employment contracts that predetermine nominal wages and let firms choose the level of employment subsequently.

Figure 3.1 shows the equilibrium in the goods market. I shall adopt the convention of requiring that the economy operate at the intersection of the supply and demand schedules. This is no more than a convention because any consid-

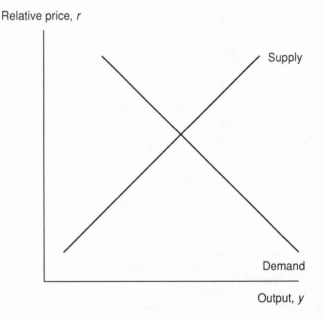

Figure 3.1   The Goods Market

erations of price rigidity or non-market-clearing can be built into the supply and demand schedules. I do not mean to suggest that the point of intersection in figure 3.1 has any of the favorable properties such as efficiency that occur in an idealized competitive equilibrium. In particular, the equilibrium in figure 3.1 may well involve underemployed labor because the supply schedule does not reflect the fundamental preferences of workers. Although the use of a supply curve in figure 3.1 suggests competition, the analysis developed here applies in noncompetitive cases as well. Absent competition, figure 3.1 should be replaced by an analysis of the joint determination of the quantity of output and the relative price. If the seller is a monopolist, for example, the analysis would presumably describe the outcome of profit maximization.

The supply and demand schedules in figure 3.1 are perturbed by the money price level, p. In addition, a vector of real determinants of output, x, shifts supply and demand. The vector x includes shifts of technology, preferences, government purchases and taxes, and noise variables. The equilibrium output in figure 3.1 can be written as a function of p and x: $y^*(p, x)$. Monetary neutrality holds when equilibrium output is independent of the price level, p. The case of nonneutrality is shown in figure 3.2. The EQ curve shows that equilibrium output level depends positively on the money price level. The EQ curve will have the same role that the aggregate supply curve does in the standard analysis. I shall stress, however, that the EQ curve is perturbed by all of the real disturbances, x. For example, the EQ curve will shift to the right if the government raises its purchases of goods. Standard analysis usually teaches that AS is a stable curve that depends only on a narrow range of factors considered by firms in setting prices and determining output.

In models with nonneutrality, consideration of the determinants of the price level is required to complete the model of output volatility. Let the money demand schedule be

Price level, p

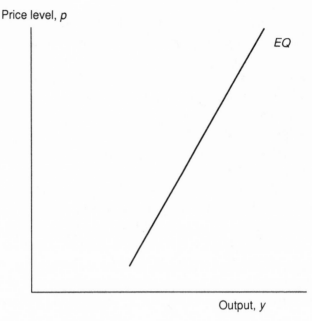

Figure 3.2   *The EQ Curve*

$$\frac{M}{p} = F(r,p,x) \ . \qquad (1.3)$$

Although it is conventional in macroeconomics to state the demand for money as a function of the level of consumption or of labor supply, the convention of general equilibrium is to put only prices on the right-hand side. In accord with the latter convention, the interest rate or other relative price, r, in $F(r, p, x)$ is not the service price of money (which is a constant determined solely by government policy); rather, the relative price is the determinant of the levels of consumption and labor supply, against which money is held. Again, the presence of p in F is a sign of monetary nonneutrality.

Define the MD curve as the combinations of p and y along which the interest rate or relative price associated with money demand is equal to the interest rate associated with product demand:

Given p, solve $\dfrac{M}{p} = F(r,p,x)$ for r and insert r into $D(r,p)$ to get y.

Note that the logic of *MD* is essentially that of finding the intersection of the *IS* curve (product demand) and the *LM* curve (money demand). In standard macroeconomic analysis, the result is the aggregate demand (AD) schedule. I think, however, that "aggregate demand" is a misleading term for *MD*, because *MD* is not the product demand function. Product demand enters the *MD* schedule only to solve out the relative price variable. It would make just as much sense to use product supply to solve out r. Monetary equilibrium is at the heart of the *MD* curve.

Figure 3.3 shows the *EQ* and *MD* curves in one diagram for the general case of monetary nonneutrality. Under the assumptions that higher prices stimulate higher supply (*S* increasing in p) and higher demand (*D* increasing in p), the *EQ* curve must slope upward. Absent strong nonneutralities in product demand or money demand, *MD* slopes downward. On the other hand, if the money price level has a positive effect on product demand, *MD* is flatter or even slopes upward. This possibility calls attention to a subtle difference between *MD* and AD. *MD* is derived from standard demand functions that are defined as the amount demanded conditional on selling endowments at the given price. AD assumes that the proceeds from sales of endowments is the variable y. At the intersection with *EQ* or AS, the two assumptions about resources available for consumption are the same, so the difference is one of definition, not substance. The definition of the AD curve, however, is confusing to the economist trained in standard general equilibrium.

The comparative statics analysis of figure 3.3 is reasonably obvious. An increase in the money stock, M, shifts *MD* to the right and raises p and y. An exogenous increase in product supply raises y and lowers p. An exogenous increase in product

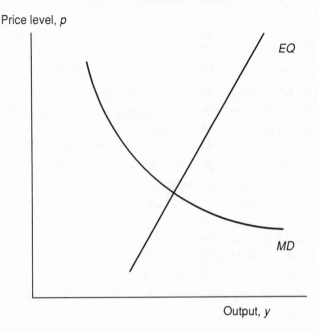

Price level, *p*

EQ

MD

Output, *y*

Figure 3.3   Equilibrium

demand shifts both *EQ* and *MD* to the right, because both schedules involve the product demand function. Output rises but the effect on price is ambiguous. The last property is the only respect in which *MD*-*EQ* differs from *AD*-*AS*. The reason is the exclusion of product demand from *AS*, as a result of the very strong assumptions underlying *AS*.

2. AGGREGATE SUPPLY AS A SPECIAL CASE OF *EQ*

The *EQ* curve is the centerpiece of the equilibrium real business cycle model, describing the level of output resulting from the equalization of product supply and demand by the real interest rate. Product demand has an equal role with product supply. But in the AD-AS literature AS is strictly a matter of supply. The student in intermediate macroeconomics learns about long-run AS as determined by the labor force and the capital stock, and about short-run AS as a Phillips curve, but gets no hint that movements in product demand might affect short-run AS.

The assumption of AS is the exclusion of the real interest rate or other relative price and the real disturbances, x, from the product supply function:

$$y = S(p) . \tag{2.1}$$

Under this assumption, $S(p)$ is the EQ curve by itself; product demand $D(r, p, x)$ simply determines r. The assumption justifies calling EQ the AS curve. Empirical evidence on real interest rates and product or labor supply is mixed and inconclusive. The evidence is strong that exogenous increases in product demand such as military buildups cause increases in output. Within the assumptions of the equilibrium real business cycle model, the evidence calls for positive real interest rate effects on product supply.

The discussion in the first two chapters shows that strong responses to changes in real interest rates are not the only mechanism capable of explaining the volatility of output. The evidence suggests that temporal agglomeration should be taken seriously in a macroeconomic model. Either intertemporal substitution is very high or thick-market effects are strong enough to overcome workers' dislike of irregular work schedules. The research of West (1986) and Ramey (1988) shows persuasively that producers accept wide fluctuations in the level of output in spite of their ability to offset these fluctuations in part through inventory accumulation and decumulation. Rather than build inventories at times when future increases in output are foreseeable and then draw inventories down when sales become strong, producers generally do the opposite. They accumulate inventories most aggressively when sales are at their peak. The only reasonable conclusion is that producers do not perceive diseconomies of production in occasional bursts. On the contrary, they appear to favor the bunching of production. Their behavior suggests increasing returns, as in the temporal agglomeration model.

If intertemporal substitution in production is high, a substantial interest-elasticity of output is indicated. Producers are indifferent to the timing of output on the cost side; when a high real interest rate rewards early sales in relation to later ones, current production should rise. If, however, the irregularity of output represents the victory of thick-market effects over preferences for smooth work schedules, the interest-elasticity of product supply need not be large. The observed relation of market real interest rates and production leaves the issue largely unresolved. The worldwide rise in real interest rates over the past decade did not coincide with any dramatic acceleration of output. I think the most favorable case for elastic supply is the following. Interpret r not as the market real interest rate but as the underlying shadow real cost of delaying production. When an increase in product demand raises that shadow cost, producers respond vigorously. The market real rate is such a poor measure of the shadow cost that the supply effect is hard to observe directly. Agency and information problems block the arbitrage of variations in the shadow cost relative to market rates.

In addition to the nonmonetary sources of fluctuations associated with intertemporal substitution and temporal agglomeration, nonneutralities in product supply, as set forth in the standard AD-AS model, are a further explanation of output volatility. At this stage, empirical decomposition of total volatility into components from intertemporal substitution, temporal agglomeration, and monetary shocks is only just underway, and opinions on the relative importance of the three components remain diverse.

3. MONETARY POLICY

Few central banks keep their portfolios on an exogenous path as assumed in the previous discussion. Instead, they react to current economic developments. A simple and broad characterization of policy is that the bank chooses a line in y-p space describing the combinations of y and p that it considers satisfactory for the period. Presumably the line slopes downward; if higher prices are to be tolerated, real activity must be depressed so as to push for lower prices or at least less inflation in the future. Call this line the MP curve. If the bank adjusts its portfolio as necessary to keep the economy on the MP curve, the MP curve takes the place of the MD curve in the analysis described earlier. Everything else remains the same.

One example of an MP curve is the rectangular hyperbola corresponding to a policy of stabilizing nominal income. In this setting, I pose the same question as at the outset: What happens to the price level and output if there is an exogenous rise in product demand? With the AS assumption, the answer is immediate. Product demand has no role in either the AS curve or the MP curve, so the price level and output must remain unchanged. With a more general EQ curve, the EQ curve will shift outward, output must rise, and the price level must fall. In an economy where it was known that central bank policy stabilized nominal income, the positive association between exogenous demand the output would be a strong indication that supply was elastic.

4. NONCOMPETITIVE EQUILIBRIUM MODELS

The analysis described earlier assumes competition in the product market, or else the concept of a supply function would not be well defined. But recent research in noncompetitive, equilibrium models is easily accommodated. Define the EQ schedule as the output resulting from the interaction of the sellers and buyers when the money price level is p. If demand arises from price takers alone, use the definition of the *MD* schedule formulated earlier. If not, it is reasonable to define the *MD* schedule in terms of the real interest rate for the same level of output on the *EQ* curve. If policy can be summarized in an *MP* curve, these questions about *MD* do not arise. In that case the comparative statics analysis proceeds as described for the competitive case. A noncompetitive economy does not have an aggregate supply curve, but it has a perfectly well-defined *EQ* curve.

5. SIMPLE FULLY DEVELOPED MODELS

In this section I shall lay out a sequence of simple models in which preferences and technology are completely spelled out. First, consider an economy with no intertemporal trading opportunities. In each period, labor can be used to produce output at a constant ratio of 1:1. Consequently, the real wage is always 1. Worker-consumers have Cobb-Douglas preferences over goods consumption, real monetary services, and leisure, with shares α, β, and $1-\alpha-\beta$, respectively. The government provides money in quantity M and charges a fixed rental price of μ per period for it. The government uses the proceeds to finance government purchases of x, with any deficit or surplus covered by a lump-sum tax or rebate.

Let z be the real proceeds from the rental of money:

$$z = \mu \, \frac{M}{p} \, . \tag{5.1}$$

The public's income after taxes is

$$1 - x + z \, , \tag{5.2}$$

and its real spending on monetary services is

$$z = \beta(1 - x + z) \,. \tag{5.3}$$

Thus

$$z = \frac{\beta}{1 - \beta} (1 - x) \,. \tag{5.4}$$

The *EQ* schedule is just the demand schedule for goods:

$$y = \alpha(1 - x + z) + x \tag{5.5}$$

$$= \frac{\alpha}{1 - \beta} + \frac{1 - \alpha - \beta}{1 - \beta} x \,.$$

This is also the labor and product supply schedule, because there is no operational relative price. Note that an increase in product demand—in the form of higher government purchases, x—shifts the *EQ* schedule to the right. This represents the operation of an income effect in labor supply.

Because there is no interest rate or other relative price determined in the goods market, the *MD* curve can be derived simply by equating money demand to money supply:

$$\frac{\beta}{1 - \beta} (1 - x) = \mu \frac{M}{p} \tag{5.6}$$

or

$$p = \frac{1 - \beta}{\beta} \frac{\mu}{1 - x} M \,. \tag{5.7}$$

The price level is proportional to the money stock and depends positively on government purchases as well. Figure 3.4 shows the vertical *EQ* and horizontal *MD* schedules. The model has monetary neutrality.

To introduce nonneutrality in the most transparent way, I shall make labor supply and product demand depend on the

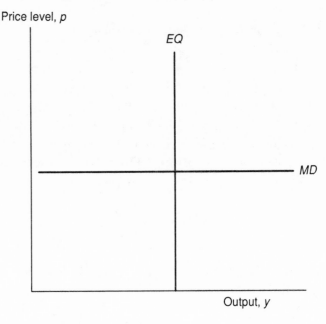

Price level, p

EQ

MD

Output, y

Figure 3.4   Equilibrium in the Example

money price level. Obviously this does not do full justice to
theories based on contractual commitments—it is closer to a
theory of money illusion. Let the share α depend on the price
level in the following way:

$$\alpha = \alpha_o \frac{p}{\bar{p}} . \tag{5.8}$$

The share is α_0 when p is at a predetermined level, $\bar{p}$, and is
higher when p is higher. People work harder and consume
more when the price level rises. Standard macroeconomics
would say the price level rises when output and employment
are high, but it comes to the same thing.

The EQ schedule in this setup is

$$y = \frac{\alpha_o \dfrac{p}{\bar{p}}}{1 - \beta} (1 - x) + x . \tag{5.9}$$

It remains true that government purchases shift *EQ* to the right through an income effect. Putting in monetary non-neutrality does not eliminate the role of the variable that was important in determining output in the case of full neutrality.

The *MD* curve is unchanged for the case of nonneutrality. Figure 3.5 shows the upward-sloping *EQ* schedule and flat *MD* schedules for the case. It shows that an increase in the quantity of money, *M*, will shift *MD* upward and raise output, thanks to the nonneutrality reflected in the slope of *EQ*.

6. INTERTEMPORAL SUBSTITUTION

I shall now consider a two-period version of the previous model with an explicit interest rate. Because there are no physical opportunities to trade between time periods, the real allocations in this model are the same as in the previous

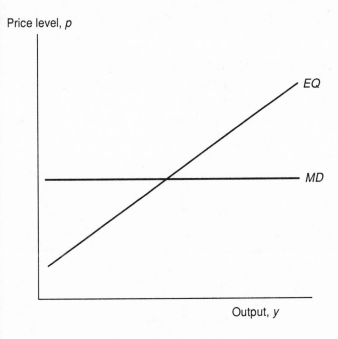

Figure 3.5   Equilibrium in the Second Example

model. The existence of a credit marker with an interest rate, however, permits an interpretation of output movements as responses to the interest rate as well as income effects. Further, the new model serves as a full illustration of the derivation of the *EQ* and *MD* schedules.

Let intertemporal utility be the sum over two periods of the log-utilities implicit in the previous model. Let R be the market discount rate: $R = 1/(1 + r)$, where r is the interest rate. Then full wealth (the value of endowments at market prices) is

$$W(R) = 1 - x_1 + z_1 + R(1 - x_2 + z_2) . \qquad (6.1)$$

Solving as before for z yields

$$z = \frac{1}{2} \frac{\beta}{1 - \beta} [1 - x_1 + R(1 - x_2)] . \qquad (6.2)$$

Full wealth is

$$z = \frac{1}{1 - \beta} [1 - x_1 + R(1 - x_2)] . \qquad (6.3)$$

The product demand schedule is

$$y = W(R) + x_1 . \qquad (6.4)$$

Demand is an increasing function of R, that is, a decreasing function of the real interest rate. The product-labor supply function is

$$y = 1 - \frac{1 - \alpha - \beta}{2} W(R) , \qquad (6.5)$$

which is an increasing function of the real interest rate. The intersection of demand and supply is exaclty as given earlier in equation 5.5. To derive the *MD* schedule, I start with the money demand function,

$$\mu \frac{M_1}{p_1} = \frac{\beta}{2} W(R) . \qquad (6.6)$$

I then use the product demand schedule, equation 6.4, to replace $W(R)$ by a function of y:

$$\mu \, \frac{M_1}{p_1} = \frac{\beta}{\alpha} (y_1 - x_1) \, , \qquad (6.7)$$

or

$$p = \frac{\alpha\mu}{\beta} \, \frac{M_1}{y_1 - x_1} \, . \qquad (6.8)$$

Note that this version of *MD* has the customary downward slope, whereas the previous version was flat. Both versions intersect *EQ* at the same price level. This one contemplates the level of output that would be demanded if the interest rate were at a level that induced individuals to seek intertemporal trades, whereas in the earlier case, individuals were aware of the impossibility of such trades. In equilibrium no intertemporal trades occur, which is why the two *MD* curves intersect *EQ* at the same point.

Nonneutrality in Product Demand

In the following example, nonneutrality in produce demand is a result of distributional effects from nominal precommitments. Firms agree in advance with their workers to provide a fixed nominal level of compensation, independent of the actual amount of work. That is, compensation is a guaranteed annual amount. The guarantee is in nominal terms because the parties view the monetary unit as the natural way to express forward obligations. Were monetary policy approximately optimal, nominal forward contracts would be correspondingly approximately optimal. The employment contract does not grant to employers the right to choose the level of employment without regard to the labor supply of the work force. Rather, employment is set at the efficient level. The effect of the nominal precommitment is to make a lump-sum transfer of wealth to management if the price level is unexpectedly high. Management places all incremental wealth in goods. Hence there is a distributional effect of the price level. A higher price level raises product demand through the assumption about management. It raises labor supply through a negative income effect. Hence a higher nominal price level raises equilibrium output. In the earlier model, there was exact proportionality between the nominal incomes of workers and the money stock. If contracts predetermine nominal incomes, then there is no freedom *ex post* for the money stock to differ from the level needed to ratify the predetermined income level. To get an interesting model, it is necessary to change the money demand assumption. A simple and standard assumption is that money is demanded in proportion to nominal GNP:

$$M = \theta p y .\qquad(6.9)$$

Under this assumption, it is unnecessary to posit any rental earnings on money by the government. The consumption share of monetary services, β, is also taken as 0.

The derivation of equilibrium output is straightforward because the stabilization of compensation by management has the same effect in the model as the taxing and spending of the government. The government makes a lump-sum transfer from workers to itself and uses all of the proceeds to purchase goods. It is only necessary to link the level of the transfer, x, to the amount of the nominal compensation commitment. If the nominal commitment is $\bar{p}$, then it is $\bar{p}/p$ in real terms. Planned real compensation is α. Actual real compensation falls in proportion to the excess of p over $\bar{p}$. Thus the employer takes back x in real terms from the workers, where

$$x = \alpha\left(1 - \frac{\bar{p}}{p}\right) .\qquad(6.10)$$

Recall that the EQ curve is

$$y = \alpha(1 - x) + x . \qquad (6.11)$$

With the transfer, x, as in equation 6.10, the nonneutral EQ curve is

$$y = \alpha[1 + (1 - \alpha)(1 - \frac{\bar{p}}{p})] . \qquad (6.12)$$

The MD curve is jut a rewriting of equation 6.9:

$$y = \frac{M}{\theta p} . \qquad (6.13)$$

Figure 3.6 shows the upward-sloping EQ curve and the downward-sloping MD curve. An increase in M raises output. Again, the mechanism is distributional—an increase in nominal demand shifts the distribution of income toward manager, because of the nominal wage commitment. Managers place all of their earnings in goods, so there is a stimulus to

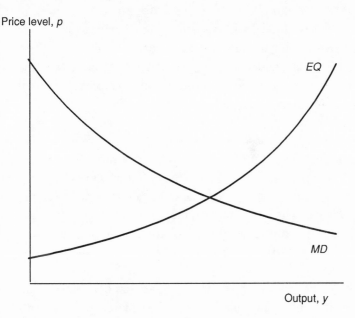

Figure 3.6   Nonneutrality in Product Demand

goods demand, which raises equilibrium output just as an increase in government purchases would.

7. CONCLUSIONS

Models of the determination of equilibrium output need not lead separate lives from models of the short run, where nominal precommitments are important. Rather, nominal influences should be built into the product supply, product demand, and money demand functions of the equilibrium model. The resulting model can accommodate a wide spectrum of views about macroeconomics. At one end is the price-rigidity model, where sellers make call-option contracts with their customers with nominal striking prices. In that model, the EQ curve simply describes the call option and is the same as the aggregate supply curve of standard expositions of price rigidity. At the other end is the real business cycle or pure equilibrium model with complete monetary neutrality. The analysis leading to the vertical EQ curve contains all the features of that model. The EQ-MD diagram shows how the price level is determined, an issue usually neglected in the real business cycle literature.

In between these two polar cases lies a wide variety of interesting macroeconomic models. The analysis of all types of noise in product or labor demand—government purchases, unpredictable agglomeration in the business sector, or shifts in consumer behavior—needs the full treatment underlying the EQ curve. The call-option hypothesis needed to justify the AS curve is too restrictive to describe the determination of total output, even if it is a helpful idea in understanding some sectors.

Analysis of monetary nonneutrality has been stagnant in recent years. The general framework that I have outlined calls attention to the great variety of ways that nonneutrality can enter a macroeconomic model. In addition to call options with nominal striking prices in product and labor markets, nominal precommitments in bonds, mortgages, dividends, and long-term employment compensation generate important nonneutralities through distributional effects.

References

Akerlof, George; Rose, Andrew; and Yellen, Janet. 1988. "Job Switching and Job Satisfaction in the U.S. Labor Market." Department of Economics, University of California Berkeley.

Barsky, Robert B., and Miron, Jeffrey A. 1989. "The Seasonal Cycle and the Business Cycle." *Journal of Political Economy* 97: 503–34.

Barsky, Robert B.; Kimball, Miles; and Warner, Elizabeth. 1988. "A Model of Weekend and Holiday Sales." Department of Economics, University of Michigan.

Bernanke, Ben S. 1983. "Non-Monetary Effects of the Financial Crisis in the Propagation of the Great Depression." *American Economic Review* 73: 257–76.

Coase, R. H. 1937. "The Nature of the Firm." *Economica* 4: 386–405.

Diamond, Peter. 1982. "Aggregate Demand Management in Search Equilibrium." *Journal of Political Economy* 90: 881–94.

Durlauf, Steven N., and Hall, Robert E. 1988. "Bounds on the Variances of Specification Errors in Models with Expectations." Department of Economics and Hoover Institution, Stanford University.

Hall, Robert E. 1988a. "Increasing Returns: Theory and Measurement with Industry Data." Hoover Institution and the Department of Economics, Stanford University.

———. 1988b. "The Relationship Between Price and Marginal Cost in U.S. Industry." *Journal of Political Economy* 96: 921–47.

LeRoy, Stephen, and Richard Porter. 1981. "The Present-Value Relation: Tests Based on Implied Variance Bounds." *Econometrica* 49: 555–74.

Lucas, Robert J. 1972. "Expectations and the Neutrality of Money." *Journal of Economic Theory* 4: 103–24.

Mankiw, N. Gregory; Romer, David; and Shapiro, Matthew D. 1985. "An Unbiased Reexamination of Stock Price Volatility." *Journal of Finance* 40: 677–87.

Murphy, Kevin M.; Shleifer, Andrei; and Vishny, Robert. 1988. "Industrialization and the Big Push." Graduate School of Business, University of Chicago.

Phelps, Edmund S. et al. 1970. *Microeconomic Foundations of Employment and Inflation Theory.* New York: W. W. Norton.

Prescott, Edward C. 1986. "Theory Ahead of Business Cycle Measurement." In *Real Business Cycles, Real Exchange Rates and Actual Policies,* vol. 25 in the *Carnegie-Rochester Conference Series on Public Policy,* ed. by Karl Brunner and Allan Meltzer. Amsterdam: North-Holland, pp. 11–44.

Ramey, Valerie A. 1988. "Non-Convex Costs and the Behavior of Inventories." Department of Economics, University of California San Diego. Unpublished paper.

Rogerson, Richard. 1988. "Indivisible Labor, Lotteries and Equilibrium." *Journal of Monetary Economics* 21: 3–16.

Shiller, Robert J. 1981. "Do Stock Prices Move Too Much to Be Justified by Subsequent Changes in Dividends?" *American Economic Review* 71: 421–36.

Tobin, James. 1965. *Money and Economic Growth."* *Econometrica* 33: 671–84.

West, Kenneth D. 1986. "A Variance Bounds Test of the Linear Quadratic Inventory Model." *Journal of Political Economy* 94: 374–401.